Teen Muscle Mastery:

Unlocking Strength

THE ULTIMATE GUIDE TO BUILDING MUSCLE, BOOSTING STRENGTH, AND STAYING FIT FOR TEENS & BEGINNERS

THE POWER OF STARTING YOUNG: BUILDING MUSCLE AS A TEEN

Building muscle as a teenager is about more than just looking good—it's about laying the foundation for a healthier, stronger, and more confident future. Starting strength training early provides lifelong benefits that go beyond the gym. As a teen, your body is primed for growth, making it the perfect time to begin focusing on your physical health and fitness. Whether you're looking to boost your athletic performance, improve your body image, or simply feel more confident in yourself, muscle building can make a significant difference.

The Long-Term Benefits of Strength Training for Teens

Improved Health and Fitness: Muscle building isn't just for bodybuilders. Strength training enhances overall fitness, helps control body weight, and reduces the risk of developing chronic diseases like obesity, heart disease, and diabetes later in life. Starting young means developing strong bones, joints, and muscles that can protect you from injury both now and in the future.

Boosted Confidence: As you begin to see results from your workouts, your self-esteem will naturally grow. Many teens struggle with body image, but working towards your fitness goals can give you a sense of control and pride over your appearance. Building muscle provides visible results that reinforce your hard work, helping you feel stronger both physically and mentally.

Better Athletic Performance: Strength training helps improve power, speed, and endurance, giving you an edge in sports and other physical activities. Many top athletes credit weight training as a key factor in their success. By building a solid strength foundation early, you're setting yourself up to excel in competitive sports or even just to enjoy physical activities more fully.

Positive Body Image: In today's world, where social media often puts pressure on teens to look a certain way, focusing on building strength rather than just aesthetics can help shift your mindset. When you start seeing the progress in your physical strength, it can lead to a more positive body image. You'll learn to appreciate what your body can *do*, not just how it looks.

Lifelong Healthy Habits: Building muscle isn't just about short-term gains—it's about creating a lifestyle. The discipline and routine you develop through strength training can translate into other areas of your life. Establishing good habits around exercise, nutrition, and recovery now will make it easier to maintain your health as you get older.

Teen Success Stories: Safe and Effective Transformations

You don't have to take our word for it—there are countless success stories of teens who have safely transformed their bodies through strength training. Take, for example, David Laid, who started working out as a skinny teenager and is now a fitness icon, inspiring millions of teens worldwide. Or Dylan McKenna, who built muscle to improve his performance in sports and later became a successful fitness coach, helping other teens reach their potential. These teens focused on safe, progressive muscle-building routines, paired with proper nutrition and rest, and they've shown that with the right approach, amazing results are possible.

Building muscle as a teenager sets the stage for success—not just in the gym, but in life. Whether you're aiming to get stronger, feel more confident, or improve your athletic abilities, now is the perfect time to get started.

CHAPTER 1: THE SCIENCE OF TEEN MUSCLE GROWTH

When you start lifting weights as a teenager, you're not just building strength for today—you're setting the stage for a lifetime of fitness. To understand how you can maximise your muscle growth during your teen years, it's essential to grasp the basic science behind how muscles grow and what makes this time in your life so unique for building strength. This chapter breaks down the process and explains why starting young can put you miles ahead when it comes to health, athletic performance, and physique development.

How Muscles Grow: The Science of Hypertrophy

At the core of muscle building is a process called hypertrophy. When you lift weights or perform resistance exercises, you're challenging your muscles. This challenge causes tiny tears in the muscle fibres. While that might sound alarming, it's actually a good thing! After your workout, your body goes into repair mode, healing those small tears and, in the process, making your muscles thicker and stronger than before. This is how muscle growth happens over time.

What's important to remember is that progression is key. You can't lift the same amount of weight, do the same exercises, or stay at the same intensity forever and expect continuous growth.

To build muscle, you need to gradually increase the challenge —whether it's by lifting heavier weights, increasing the number of reps, or trying more difficult exercises. This concept is called progressive overload, and it's the foundation of long-term muscle growth.

Puberty: Your Secret Muscle-Building Weapon

Here's where being a teenager gives you an edge over adults: your body is naturally primed for growth thanks to puberty. During this phase of your life, your body releases a surge of hormones like testosterone and growth hormone. These hormones are crucial for building muscle, which is why it's easier to see rapid progress during your teen years compared to later in life.

Testosterone, in particular, plays a big role in muscle development. This hormone helps your body synthesise protein, which is the building block of muscle. While testosterone is higher in males, both males and females experience hormonal changes during puberty that boost muscle growth potential. This means that if you start lifting now, you're taking full advantage of your body's natural muscle-building abilities.

By starting young, you can harness these hormonal benefits and set a strong foundation for the future. The muscle and strength you build as a teen will make it easier for you to maintain and build on that progress later in life, even when hormone levels begin to stabilise.

Recovery and Sleep: The Hidden Keys to Growth

One of the biggest mistakes young lifters make is thinking that more is always better. It's easy to get caught up in wanting quick results, but pushing yourself too hard without enough rest can actually slow down your progress. Here's why: muscles don't grow in the gym—they grow during recovery.

When you lift weights, you're breaking down muscle fibres, but the actual growth happens after your workout, during rest. This makes recovery time just as important as the workout itself. You need to give your body time to heal and rebuild stronger muscles. If you don't rest enough, you risk overtraining, which can lead to injury and burnout.

One of the most powerful tools for recovery is something you're already doing every day: sleep. During sleep, your body releases growth hormone and other critical substances that help repair and build muscle tissue. For teens, sleep is even more important because your body is growing at a rapid rate, and muscle recovery is part of that process. Aim for at least 8-10 hours of sleep per night to maximise your muscle gains and overall well-being.

Teens vs. Adults: Why You're in the Best Position to Build Muscle

While adults can certainly build muscle, they don't have the same advantages as teens when it comes to making fast progress. There are a few key differences between teen and adult bodies when it comes to strength training:

Higher Growth Potential: As mentioned earlier, puberty puts you in a prime muscle-building window due to elevated levels of hormones like testosterone and growth hormone. Adults, especially those past their early 20s, don't have these natural boosts anymore.

Faster Recovery: Teenagers generally recover more quickly from workouts than adults. Your body is more resilient, meaning you can handle more frequent training sessions without getting as sore or needing as much recovery time as an older adult.

Long-Term Gains: When you start strength training young, you're not just building muscle for today—you're setting the foundation for future progress. Muscle has memory, so the work you put in now will make it easier to stay fit and strong as you get older. Lifelong habits formed during your teen years are easier to maintain and build upon, giving you a significant advantage over someone who starts lifting later in life.

The Importance of Progression: Small Steps, Big Results

One of the biggest lessons in muscle building is that slow and steady wins the race. While it might be tempting to lift as much weight as possible right off the bat, starting with proper form and gradually increasing your weights is crucial. This concept of progression will keep you on track for long-term success.

Each time you challenge your muscles with a little more weight, an extra rep, or a tougher exercise, you're forcing them to adapt and grow. Consistent, gradual increases lead to sustainable progress without the risk of injury or burnout. Remember, muscle building isn't an overnight process. It's about showing up, putting in the work, and letting your body adapt over time.

Why Starting Young Will Help You for Life

By beginning your strength training journey now, you're setting yourself up for lifelong success. The muscle and habits you build as a teenager will benefit you for years to come, from better athletic performance and injury prevention to improved mental health and confidence. And as you get older, staying fit and healthy will be much easier if you've already laid a strong foundation.

Muscle building is more than just lifting weights—it's about creating a disciplined routine, understanding how your body works, and making the most of this prime time for growth. So don't rush the process; embrace it. You're in one of the best phases of your life to start building the body—and the mindset—you want.

CHAPTER 2: BUILDING A SOLID FOUNDATION

Before you dive into lifting heavy weights or hitting the gym hard, it's crucial to build a strong foundation. Think of it like constructing a house—you wouldn't start with the roof before laying down solid ground. In strength training, that foundation comes from mastering bodyweight exercises, developing core strength, and ensuring proper form. By focusing on these key areas, you'll not only build muscle but also protect yourself from injury and set the stage for long-term success in fitness.

This chapter will show you how to start strength training the right way, giving you the tools to master your body before you move on to heavier challenges.

Bodyweight Exercises: The Starting Point for Strength

Bodyweight exercises are your best friend when you're first starting out. They may not look as impressive as bench pressing or deadlifting, but don't underestimate how effective they can be. These exercises use the weight of your own body to build muscle, improve coordination, and enhance your overall fitness. Plus, they can be done anywhere—no fancy gym equipment required!

Here are some of the essential bodyweight exercises that every beginner should focus on:

Push-Ups: A classic, and for good reason. Push-ups work your chest, shoulders, triceps, and core all at once. Plus, there are tons of variations to keep them challenging as you progress. Start with a focus on perfect form—keep your body in a straight line, elbows tucked slightly, and lower yourself with control.

Pull-Ups: Pull-ups are one of the best exercises for developing upper body strength, particularly in your back, shoulders, and arms. Don't worry if you can't do one yet—start by hanging from the bar to build grip strength or use a band for assistance. It'll come with time and practice.

Squats: Squats are a must for building lower body strength, working your quads, hamstrings, glutes, and even your core. Whether you're doing bodyweight squats or goblet squats with light weights, mastering this movement is critical for all kinds of sports and daily activities.

Planks: A great exercise for core stability, planks help strengthen your abs, lower back, and shoulders. Hold a plank position with your body straight, elbows beneath your shoulders, and hold for as long as possible without losing form.

The beauty of bodyweight exercises is that they engage multiple muscle groups at once, helping you build functional strength. Once you've mastered these, you can gradually introduce more challenging variations or incorporate weights to keep progressing.

Core Strength: The Center of All Movement

You've probably heard people say, "Strength comes from the core," and they're right. A strong core is essential for almost every physical movement you make, whether it's lifting weights, running, or even sitting upright. Your core includes your abs, lower back, obliques, and the deeper muscles that stabilise your spine.

Focusing on core strength will help you:

Prevent injuries: A strong core stabilises your body during exercises, reducing the risk of injury, especially to your lower back.

Enhance your posture: Good core strength helps you stand tall and maintain proper posture, which not only makes you look more confident but also reduces strain on your body.

Improve balance and coordination: A stable core helps you maintain balance during exercises like squats, deadlifts, and even athletic movements like jumping or sprinting.

Here are some simple but effective core exercises to incorporate into your routine:

Dead Bugs: Lie on your back with your arms straight up and your knees bent at 90 degrees. Slowly lower one arm and the opposite leg toward the floor while keeping your lower back pressed into the ground. Return to the starting position and switch sides.

Bird Dogs: Start on your hands and knees. Extend one arm and the opposite leg straight out, keeping your hips level. Return to the starting position and repeat on the other side. This is great for core stability and balance.

Leg Raises: Lie flat on your back with your legs straight. Slowly raise your legs to a 90-degree angle and then lower them without letting them touch the ground. This engages your lower abs and hip flexors.

A strong core is like having a powerful engine for your body—it makes everything else you do, whether it's lifting weights or playing sports, that much more effective.

The Importance of Posture, Balance, and Flexibility

When you're young, it's easy to think you're invincible. But without good posture, balance, and flexibility, you're setting yourself up for injuries that can sideline your progress. These might not be the most glamorous aspects of fitness, but they're crucial for long-term success.

Posture: Good posture doesn't just make you look more confident—it's essential for lifting weights properly and safely. Poor posture can lead to muscle imbalances, which increase your risk of injury. Focus on keeping your shoulders back, chest lifted, and spine in a neutral position during all exercises.

Balance: Balance is critical for exercises like squats and lunges. If you lack balance, you'll struggle to maintain proper form, which can lead to injury. Start with exercises like single-leg squats or lunges to improve your balance over time.

Flexibility: Flexible muscles and joints move better, which helps you avoid injury and improve your performance. Stretching regularly, especially after workouts, will keep your muscles loose and ready for action. Key areas to focus on include your hamstrings, hip flexors, and shoulders.

Building flexibility and balance now will pay off in the long run, making it easier to progress to more challenging exercises and lifting heavier weights without risking injury.

Mastering Technique Before Adding Weight

It's easy to get excited about lifting heavier and heavier, but here's the truth: if your technique isn't on point, you're putting yourself at serious risk of injury. Lifting with poor form not only hurts your progress but can also lead to long-term problems like joint pain or muscle strains.

Here are a few tips to **master your technique** before adding weights:

Start with bodyweight: Before grabbing dumbbells or barbells, make sure you can perform exercises like squats, lunges, and push-ups with perfect form. This will ensure that you've built the necessary strength and coordination.

Watch your posture: Keep your core tight, back straight, and shoulders engaged during exercises. Avoid rounding your back during movements like squats or deadlifts.

Use mirrors or film yourself: A mirror can help you check your form in real time, while recording yourself will allow you to spot mistakes you may not notice during your workout.

Don't rush: Slow, controlled movements are better for building strength and avoiding injury than fast, sloppy reps. Focus on quality over quantity.

Once you've mastered bodyweight exercises with good form, you can start to add light weights and progressively challenge yourself. Remember, strength training is a marathon, not a sprint —taking the time to learn the basics now will help you progress faster and more safely in the long run.

CHAPTER 3: CREATING YOUR FIRST GYM ROUTINE

Now that you understand the science behind muscle growth and have built a solid foundation with bodyweight exercises, it's time to take things to the next level by creating your first gym routine. A well-structured workout plan is key to making consistent progress, avoiding plateaus, and staying injury-free.

In this chapter, we'll walk you through how to build a balanced routine that fits your fitness goals, focusing on essential exercises, proper rep and set ranges, and how to apply progressive overload—the key to getting stronger over time.

Full-Body vs. Split Routines: Which Is Better for Beginners?

When starting out, you'll want to choose between two common workout structures: full-body routines or split routines. Each has its own benefits, and the best choice depends on your schedule and goals.

Full-Body Routines: In a full-body routine, you work all major muscle groups in a single workout. This type of routine is ideal for beginners because it allows you to hit each muscle group multiple times per week, which is great for building a solid base of strength. Full-body workouts also save time and are usually done 2-3 times a week, leaving plenty of time for recovery.

Split Routines: In a split routine, you divide your workouts by muscle groups (e.g., upper body one day, lower body the next). While split routines are great for more advanced lifters, they can be overwhelming for beginners because they require more frequent gym sessions. If you can only work out a few times a week, a full-body routine will give you more bang for your buck.

For most teens and beginner lifters, a full-body routine is the best place to start. It allows you to build a strong foundation of strength across all your muscles and focus on mastering key movements.

The Best Beginner Exercises

When building your gym routine, stick to compound movements —exercises that work multiple muscle groups at once. These movements not only build strength more efficiently but also teach you how to move your body in a coordinated way, which will be helpful as you progress. Here are some of the most effective exercises to include in your beginner routine:

BENCH PRESS

The bench press is a staple chest exercise that also works your shoulders and triceps. It's often seen as a strength benchmark, but it's crucial to perform it with the right form to avoid injury.

How to Perform the Bench Press:

Set up: Lie flat on a bench with your feet planted firmly on the ground. Your eyes should be directly under the barbell. Grip the bar slightly wider than shoulder-width apart.

Lowering the weight: Unrack the bar and slowly lower it to your mid-chest. Your elbows should be at about a 45-degree angle to your torso, not flared out wide.

Pressing: Once the bar reaches your chest, push the weight back up while keeping your back slightly arched and your core engaged. Don't lock out your elbows at the top.

Form tips: Keep your feet on the floor and your lower back slightly arched to maintain stability. Don't bounce the bar off your chest; the movement should be controlled.

Alternatives & Variations:

Dumbbell Bench Press: This version gives you more range of motion and helps to address any strength imbalances between your arms.

Floor Press: If you don't have a bench, you can do the floor press. Lie on the floor and press a barbell or dumbbells, which limits the range of motion but still works the chest and triceps.

Push-Ups: If you don't have weights or a bench, push-ups are an excellent bodyweight alternative that mimics the pressing movement of the bench press.

SQUATS

Squats are the foundation of most strength training programs because they hit multiple muscles, including the quads, hamstrings, glutes, and core. Whether you use your body weight or a barbell, squats are essential for building lower-body strength and full-body coordination.

How to Perform a Squat:

Starting position: Stand with your feet shoulder-width apart, toes slightly pointed out. Keep your chest up and engage your core.

Lowering into the squat: Push your hips back as if you're sitting in a chair. Your knees should track over your toes but not push past them. Lower yourself until your thighs are at least parallel to the ground (or as low as you can comfortably go).

Rising up: Push through your heels to stand back up, making sure your chest stays lifted and your knees stay aligned with your toes.

Form tips: Avoid rounding your lower back—maintain a neutral spine throughout the movement. Keep your weight in your heels to avoid stressing your knees.

Alternatives & Variations:

Goblet Squat: Hold a dumbbell or kettlebell at your chest to add resistance while keeping your form in check.

Bodyweight Squats: For those without access to weights, bodyweight squats are still highly effective. Focus on perfecting your form and gradually increasing reps.

Split Squats: A great variation that focuses more on unilateral (one leg at a time) strength, which helps improve balance and muscle coordination.

DEADLIFTS

Deadlifts are one of the best exercises for developing overall body strength, targeting the posterior chain (lower back, glutes, hamstrings). However, they require precise form, as doing them incorrectly can strain your lower back.

How to Perform a Deadlift:

Set up: Stand with your feet hip-width apart, toes under the barbell. Bend your knees slightly and hinge at your hips to grip the bar just outside your knees.

Lift: With a straight back, drive through your heels to lift the bar. Keep it close to your shins as you stand up. Your chest should rise at the same rate as your hips.

Lockout: At the top, stand tall with your chest up and shoulders back. Avoid leaning backward.

Lowering the weight: Hinge at your hips again and lower the bar back to the ground, keeping your back straight.

Form tips: Engage your core throughout the movement. Don't round your back, and make sure you're lifting with your legs, not just your back.

Alternatives & Variations:

Romanian Deadlifts: Focuses more on the hamstrings and glutes, and can be done with dumbbells or a barbell.

Kettlebell Deadlifts: For beginners or those without access to a barbell, a kettlebell is a great alternative.

Trap Bar Deadlifts: Using a trap bar (hex bar) can make deadlifts easier on the lower back and help beginners maintain better form.

OVERHEAD PRESS

The overhead press works your shoulders, triceps, and core, and it's great for building upper-body strength. This exercise requires good form to prevent shoulder strain.

How to Perform an Overhead Press:

Set up: Stand with your feet shoulder-width apart, gripping the barbell just outside your shoulders. Your hands should be just outside your shoulder-width.

Pressing: Engage your core and press the barbell overhead, ensuring the weight moves in a straight line above your head.

Lockout: At the top, your arms should be fully extended but not locked out. Your head should naturally move forward so the bar is directly over your body.

Lowering the weight: Slowly lower the bar back to your shoulders, keeping your core tight to avoid arching your lower back.

Form tips: Keep your core engaged throughout the movement to prevent leaning backward.

Alternatives & Variations:

Dumbbell Overhead Press: Using dumbbells can help with mobility and balance, especially if you have limited shoulder flexibility.

Seated Overhead Press: A seated version reduces the need for core stability and focuses more on shoulder strength.

Pike Push-Ups: If you don't have weights, pike push-ups are a great bodyweight alternative that mimics the pressing motion, targeting the shoulders.

PULL-UPS

Pull-ups are a fantastic exercise for your back, shoulders, and arms, but they can be tough for beginners. However, they're incredibly rewarding once mastered.

How to Perform a Pull-Up:

Grip the bar: Use an overhand grip, with your hands slightly wider than shoulder-width apart.

Pulling up: Engage your back muscles and pull yourself up until your chin clears the bar. Avoid using momentum or swinging your legs.

Lowering down: Lower yourself back down slowly, fully extending your arms before starting the next rep.

Form tips: Focus on using your back muscles to pull, not just your arms. Keep your core tight and legs stable to avoid swinging.

Alternatives & Variations:

Assisted Pull-Ups: Use a resistance band or an assisted pull-up machine to help if you're unable to do a full pull-up yet.

Negative Pull-Ups: Jump up to the top position and slowly lower yourself down. This helps build strength needed for full pull-ups.

Inverted Rows: A great exercise for those who can't do pull-ups yet, where you hang under a barbell and pull your chest up to the bar.

ROWS

Rows are essential for developing a strong back and improving posture. They target the upper and middle back, shoulders, and arms.

How to Perform a Row:

Set up: Stand with your feet shoulder-width apart, holding a barbell or dumbbells. Bend your knees slightly and hinge at your hips so your torso is angled about 45 degrees forward.

Rowing: Pull the weight toward your torso, squeezing your shoulder blades together at the top of the movement.

Lowering the weight: Slowly lower the weight back down, keeping control throughout the movement.

Form tips: Keep your back straight and avoid rounding your shoulders. Focus on pulling with your back muscles, not just your arms.

Alternatives & Variations:

Dumbbell Rows: A great alternative to barbell rows that allows you to work each side independently.

Inverted Rows: Use a barbell set in a squat rack. Hang under the bar and pull your chest up, keeping your body in a straight line.

T-Bar Rows: A machine or barbell variation that puts more focus on the middle back, which can help with strength imbalances.

By mastering these exercises with good form and using the variations or alternatives when necessary, you'll be well on your way to building muscle and strength—whether you have access to a fully equipped gym or just a few pieces of equipment at home.

How to Progressively Overload: Getting Stronger Safely

Progressive overload is the key to continuous muscle growth. To keep making gains, you need to gradually increase the amount of stress you place on your muscles over time. Here's how to do it safely:

Add Weight: The most straightforward way to apply progressive overload is to gradually increase the weight you're lifting. Start by adding 5-10 pounds to the bar once you can comfortably complete your reps with good form.

Increase Reps: Another option is to increase the number of reps you perform for each set. For example, if you're doing 8 reps of an exercise, try moving up to 10 reps once it feels easy.

Increase Sets: You can also add more sets to your workout. For example, if you're doing 3 sets of an exercise, increase it to 4 sets once you've built enough strength.

Slow Down the Movement: Controlling the tempo of your reps—especially during the lowering (eccentric) phase—puts more strain on your muscles and makes the exercise more challenging without adding extra weight.

The key to progressive overload is to increase difficulty gradually. You don't need to jump up in weight every session, and it's important to listen to your body to avoid overtraining.

Sample 3-Day and 5-Day Workout Plans

Here are two beginner-friendly workout plans you can follow, depending on how often you want to hit the gym:

3-Day Full-Body Routine (For Beginners)
This plan hits all major muscle groups and allows for plenty of recovery time.

Day 1

- Squats: 3 sets of 8-10 reps
- Bench Press: 3 sets of 8-10 reps
- Pull-Ups (or Lat Pulldown): 3 sets of 6-8 reps
- Plank: 3 sets, hold for 30-45 seconds

Day 2

- Deadlifts: 3 sets of 6-8 reps
- Overhead Press: 3 sets of 8-10 reps
- Dumbbell Rows: 3 sets of 8-10 reps
- Leg Raises: 3 sets of 10-12 reps

Day 3

- Lunges: 3 sets of 8-10 reps (each leg)
- Incline Dumbbell Press: 3 sets of 8-10 reps
- Barbell Curls: 3 sets of 8-10 reps
- Russian Twists: 3 sets of 10-12 reps

5-Day Split Routine (For More Advanced Beginners)
This plan focuses on different muscle groups each day for more targeted training.

Day 1: Chest & Triceps

- Bench Press: 4 sets of 8-10 reps
- Incline Dumbbell Press: 3 sets of 8-10 reps

- Tricep Dips: 3 sets of 8-10 reps

Day 2: Back & Biceps

- Deadlifts: 4 sets of 6-8 reps
- Pull-Ups: 3 sets of 6-8 reps
- Barbell Rows: 3 sets of 8-10 reps

Day 3: Legs

- Squats: 4 sets of 8-10 reps
- Lunges: 3 sets of 8-10 reps (each leg)
- Leg Curls: 3 sets of 10-12 reps

Day 4: Shoulders

- Overhead Press: 4 sets of 8-10 reps
- Lateral Raises: 3 sets of 10-12 reps
- Face Pulls: 3 sets of 10-12 reps

Day 5: Core & Abs

- Planks: 3 sets, hold for 30-60 seconds
- Russian Twists: 3 sets of 12-15 reps
- Hanging Leg Raises: 3 sets of 10-12 reps

CHAPTER 4: FUELING YOUR MUSCLE GROWTH: NUTRITION BASICS

Building muscle isn't just about what you do in the gym—what you eat plays a massive role in how your body responds to your workouts. For teens especially, nutrition is essential for both overall health and muscle growth. In this chapter, we'll break down the basics of what you need to eat to maximise your gains, explaining the role of macronutrients, proper hydration, and providing some easy meal ideas to help fuel your body.

Macronutrients: What Are They, and Why Do Teens Need Them for Muscle Building?

To grow muscle effectively, your body needs three main types of nutrients—macronutrients: protein, carbohydrates, and fats. Each plays a specific role in your body's ability to repair and grow muscle, fuel your workouts, and maintain overall health.

Protein: Protein is often called the building block of muscle, and it's essential for muscle repair and growth. Every time you work out, you're creating tiny tears in your muscle fibres. Protein helps to rebuild these fibres stronger than before. Teens, in particular, need more protein because your body is already growing due to puberty.

Carbohydrates: Carbs are your body's primary source of energy, especially for intense activities like lifting weights or playing sports. They provide the fuel you need to push through tough workouts. Eating enough carbs also spares protein, allowing it to focus on muscle repair instead of being used for energy.

Fats: Healthy fats support hormone production, including testosterone, which plays a key role in muscle growth for both boys and girls. Fats also provide long-lasting energy and help absorb certain vitamins that are crucial for recovery.

Quick Nutrition Tip: A balanced diet includes all three macronutrients—protein, carbs, and fats—working together. Skipping any of them could slow down your muscle gains or affect your energy levels.

How Much Protein Should Teens Eat to Build Muscle?

Protein is vital, but how much should you actually be eating to grow muscle?

A good guideline for teens aiming to build muscle is about 0.8 to 1 gram of protein per pound of body weight per day. So, if you weigh 150 pounds, you should aim to eat 120-150 grams of protein each day. This might sound like a lot, but spreading your intake across meals and snacks makes it easier to hit your goal.

Here are some high-protein foods that are great for muscle building:

- **Chicken breast**: 25-30 grams of protein per 4-ounce serving
- **Greek yoghourt**: 15-20 grams of protein per cup
- **Eggs**: 6-7 grams of protein per egg
- **Lean beef**: 20-25 grams of protein per 4-ounce serving
- **Protein shakes**: 20-30 grams of protein per serving

If you don't eat meat or dairy, you can still get enough protein from plant-based sources like:

- **Tofu or tempeh**: 10-20 grams of protein per serving
- **Lentils and beans**: 15-18 grams of protein per cup
- **Quinoa**: 8 grams of protein per cup

Quick Protein Snack Ideas:

- Hard-boiled eggs and whole wheat toast
- Greek yoghourt with berries and honey
- Peanut butter and banana sandwich on whole-grain bread
- Protein smoothies with whey or plant-based protein powder, banana, and almond butter

Healthy Snack and Meal Ideas for Muscle Gain

Eating enough calories to fuel muscle growth is just as important as getting the right macronutrients. Active teens need extra energy, so don't be afraid to eat plenty, but make sure you're choosing nutrient-rich foods that support your goals.

Sample Meal Ideas:

- **Breakfast**: Scrambled eggs with spinach and cheese, whole-grain toast, and a glass of milk or a protein smoothie with oats and berries.
- **Lunch**: Grilled chicken sandwich on whole wheat bread, with avocado and a side of sweet potatoes or quinoa.
- **Dinner**: Baked salmon, brown rice, and roasted vegetables like broccoli and carrots.
- **Snacks**: Greek yoghourt with almonds and honey, a protein bar, apple slices with peanut butter, or hummus with whole-grain crackers.

DIY Tip: If you don't always have access to specific ingredients, keep it simple. For example, oats, eggs, and peanut butter are versatile, inexpensive, and protein-rich staples that you can turn into quick meals or snacks.

Importance of Hydration and Electrolytes

Hydration is one of the most overlooked aspects of building muscle. Water is crucial for almost every function in your body, including muscle repair, digestion, and energy production. Dehydration can not only decrease your performance in the gym but also slow down your muscle recovery.

For active teens, drinking water consistently throughout the day is essential. Aim for at least 8-10 cups (2-2.5 litres) of water daily, and more if you're working out hard or sweating a lot. In addition to water, electrolytes like sodium, potassium, and magnesium help keep your body in balance, especially after intense exercise.

Quick Hydration Tips:

- Drink water before, during, and after your workouts.
- Add a pinch of salt to your water or have a sports drink after long, sweaty sessions to replenish electrolytes.
- Coconut water is a natural source of electrolytes if you're looking for an alternative to processed sports drinks.

Sample Meal Plans and Easy-to-Follow Recipes

Here's a simple 1-day meal plan to help you start fueling your muscle growth. It focuses on balance and includes foods that most teens can access easily.

Breakfast:

- 3 scrambled eggs with spinach
- Whole-grain toast
- 1 cup of milk or a protein shake

Snack:

- Greek yoghourt with a handful of almonds

- 1 banana

Lunch:

- Grilled chicken wrap with avocado, lettuce, and tomato on a whole-wheat tortilla
- 1 apple

Snack:

- Peanut butter on whole-grain crackers or rice cakes
- A handful of baby carrots

Dinner:

- Grilled or baked salmon (or tofu for a plant-based option)
- Brown rice
- Steamed broccoli and carrots

Post-Workout Snack (optional):

A smoothie made with whey or plant-based protein powder, almond milk, a banana, and a spoonful of peanut butter

Easy Recipe: Protein-Packed Smoothie
Ingredients:

- 1 scoop of protein powder (whey or plant-based)
- 1 cup of almond milk or regular milk
- 1 banana
- 1 spoonful of peanut butter
- Handful of spinach (optional)
- 1/2 cup of oats (for extra carbs)

Blend everything together for a quick and delicious snack that's perfect for post-workout recovery or a meal on the go.

By understanding how to fuel your body with the right

macronutrients, staying hydrated, and making smart food choices, you'll give your muscles the nutrients they need to grow. Combine these nutritional habits with a solid workout routine, and you'll be well on your way to achieving your muscle-building goals.

CHAPTER 5: THE MENTAL GAME: BUILDING CONFIDENCE AND DISCIPLINE

Building muscle isn't just a physical challenge—it's a mental game, too. While lifting weights and pushing your body to new limits is important, your mindset is what will keep you on track and help you push through tough days. In this chapter, we'll explore how strength training can boost your confidence, ways to stay motivated, and how to develop the discipline needed for long-term success. We'll also address the unique body image challenges many teens face as they start their fitness journey.

How Strength Training Can Boost Confidence and Self-Esteem

Lifting weights and watching your body transform has a direct impact on your confidence. Strength training does more than just make you physically stronger; it helps you feel better about yourself on multiple levels:

1. **Physical Achievement**: Every time you lift a heavier weight or complete a tough workout, you prove to yourself that you're capable of growth and improvement. These small victories add up, making

you more confident in your abilities—not just in the gym, but in life.
2. **Body Awareness**: Strength training teaches you to connect with your body in a way few other activities can. As you become more aware of what your body is capable of, you'll likely feel more proud of your progress and less focused on superficial flaws.
3. **Positive Mindset**: Exercise releases endorphins—"feel-good" chemicals that naturally improve your mood. Over time, this can help reduce stress, anxiety, and even feelings of depression, contributing to a healthier, more positive outlook on life.

Confidence Tip: Focus on what your body can do, not just what it looks like. When you're proud of how much stronger or faster you're getting, you'll find that confidence follows naturally.

Staying Motivated: Setting Goals and Tracking Progress

Staying motivated to work out regularly, especially as a beginner, can be tough. Sometimes progress feels slow, and life gets in the way. That's why it's so important to have a solid plan for staying motivated.

1. **Set SMART Goals**: One of the most effective ways to stay on track is by setting **SMART goals**—specific, measurable, achievable, relevant, and time-bound. Instead of saying, "I want to build muscle," a SMART goal would be, "I want to add 10 pounds to my bench press in the next 8 weeks." This gives you a clear target and a timeline to work toward.
2. **Track Your Progress**: Whether it's in a journal, a workout app, or a simple notebook, tracking your progress can keep you motivated. Document your workouts, including the weights you lift and how many reps you complete. When you see that you're

getting stronger week by week, it will fuel your desire to keep going.
3. **Celebrate Small Wins**: It's easy to get discouraged if you're only focused on long-term goals. Instead, celebrate smaller milestones—like hitting a new personal best on an exercise or sticking to your workout schedule for a month. Recognizing these wins keeps you excited and motivated.
4. **Visualize Success**: Imagine how great you'll feel when you reach your goal. Visualizing your success can help keep you motivated when you're feeling sluggish or unmotivated. It reminds you why you're working so hard in the first place.

Motivation Tip: Don't focus solely on the destination—enjoy the journey. Every step you take, every workout you complete, is moving you closer to your goals. Take pride in the process.

Dealing with Body Image Struggles as a Teen Lifter

Body image can be a major concern for many teens, especially those starting their fitness journey. You might feel pressure to look a certain way or compare yourself to others, which can be tough when you're not seeing immediate results. It's important to understand that muscle building takes time, and everyone's body responds differently to training.

1. **Avoid Comparisons**: With social media constantly showcasing perfectly edited physiques, it's easy to compare yourself to others. Remember, everyone's fitness journey is unique. Your friend may gain muscle faster, or you may have strengths they don't. Focus on **your own progress**, not someone else's highlights.
2. **Be Patient**: Muscle growth is a gradual process. You won't look like a fitness model overnight. The key is

to be consistent and patient with your workouts and nutrition. If you're doing the work, the results will come.
3. **Positive Self-Talk**: How you speak to yourself matters. Instead of focusing on what you don't like about your body, focus on what you're proud of. Whether it's how much stronger you've gotten or how much effort you've put into your workouts, shifting your mindset to positivity will boost your self-esteem.
4. **Appreciate the Process**: Remember that building muscle isn't just about appearance. It's about becoming healthier, stronger, and more disciplined. If you focus on those things, body image struggles will have less power over you.

Body Image Tip: Remind yourself that you're in this for the long game. Appreciate what your body can do and how it's improving over time. Fitness isn't about perfection; it's about progress.

Building a Long-Term Mindset for Fitness Success

The key to real, lasting success in fitness is having a long-term mindset. It's not just about getting results fast—it's about building habits that you can stick with for life. Here's how you can cultivate discipline and stay committed for the long haul:

1. **Think Long-Term**: Don't view fitness as a short-term project. Instead, see it as a lifelong journey. Whether you're aiming to get stronger, leaner, or more athletic, there's no finish line. Your goals will evolve as you grow, but the habits you build now will stick with you.
2. **Discipline Over Motivation**: Motivation is great, but it comes and goes. What's more important is discipline—doing the work even when you don't

feel like it. Over time, these disciplined habits will become second nature, and you'll rely less on bursts of motivation.
3. **Stay Flexible**: Life happens. You'll have off days or weeks when you can't work out as much as you'd like. That's okay. The key is to stay flexible and not give up when things don't go perfectly. Get back on track as soon as you can, and don't be too hard on yourself.
4. **Avoid Burnout**: Going too hard, too fast can lead to burnout, especially for teens who are eager to see results. Remember to take rest days, listen to your body, and enjoy other hobbies outside the gym. Balance is important for long-term success.

Discipline Tip: Set small, daily habits that support your fitness goals, like drinking enough water, prepping your meals, or doing a quick stretch routine each morning. These habits build consistency and make sticking to your routine easier.

YOUR FITNESS JOURNEY STARTS IN THE MIND

Building muscle and staying fit is as much a mental challenge as it is a physical one. When you master the mental game—whether it's developing discipline, managing body image struggles, or staying motivated—everything else falls into place. Confidence, strength, and long-term fitness success come from developing the right mindset and sticking with it. Remember, fitness is a journey, and your biggest competition is yourself.

Stay patient, stay consistent, and most importantly, keep believing in your ability to improve. Your mind is your most powerful muscle—train it, and everything else will follow.

CHAPTER 6: STRENGTH TRAINING MYTHS BUSTED

There's a lot of misinformation out there about strength training, especially for teens. You might have heard that lifting weights will stunt your growth or that you'll get bulky overnight if you pick up a dumbbell. These myths can confuse or even discourage beginners from starting their muscle-building journey. In this chapter, we'll clear up some of the most common misconceptions about weightlifting for teens and help you separate fact from fiction.

Debunking the Myth That Weightlifting Stunts Growth

One of the biggest and most persistent myths about teen weightlifting is the idea that it stunts growth. Many worry that lifting weights will damage growth plates—the areas of soft cartilage at the ends of long bones where growth occurs during adolescence. The fear is that injuries to these areas could limit height potential.

However, research has shown that weightlifting, when done with proper form and supervision, does not stunt growth. In fact, strength training can actually support healthy development by strengthening bones, improving posture, and promoting better body mechanics. Growth plates are vulnerable to injury in any sport—whether it's weightlifting, soccer, or basketball—but with the right technique and progressive overload, weightlifting is just as safe as any other physical activity.

The Bottom Line: Lifting weights won't make you shorter. In fact, strength training can improve your posture and help you grow into a stronger, healthier version of yourself. Focus on learning proper form and starting with lighter weights to minimise the risk of injury.

Myth: Teens Will "Bulk Up" Too Fast

Another common fear is that lifting weights will make you "bulk up" too quickly, leading to an overly muscular look that some teens might not be aiming for. But the truth is, building muscle takes time, effort, and a carefully planned diet.

For teens, especially those new to strength training, it's important to understand that muscle growth is a slow, gradual process. It typically takes months—if not years—of consistent training and proper nutrition to build significant muscle mass. While you may start to feel stronger after just a few weeks, visible muscle growth happens more slowly, and you won't suddenly wake up looking like a bodybuilder.

What's more, teens' bodies are still developing, and many won't produce enough testosterone (the hormone responsible for muscle growth) to "bulk up" quickly. Instead, expect to see gradual improvements in muscle definition and strength over time.

The Reality: Muscle growth is a long-term process. You won't become too bulky overnight, so don't worry about lifting weights making you look like a pro bodybuilder too soon. If you want to build muscle without excessive bulk, focus on maintaining a balanced workout routine and diet.

Balancing Strength Training with Sports and Other Activities

Some teens worry that strength training will take up too much time or interfere with their performance in other sports. But the truth is, strength training can actually improve your athletic performance, making you stronger, faster, and more resilient in whatever sport you play.

Whether you're into soccer, basketball, swimming, or track, adding strength training to your routine can help you:

Boost power and speed: Stronger muscles allow you to move faster and perform more explosively in sports.

Improve endurance: Strength training improves your overall conditioning, helping you last longer during games or matches.

Prevent injuries: Strong muscles and joints are more stable and less prone to injury. Training your core and stabilising muscles, in particular, helps protect your body during physical activities.

The key is to balance your strength training with your other activities. If you're already heavily involved in sports, 2-3 strength sessions per week might be enough to see progress without overloading your schedule. And if you're concerned about how strength training might affect your performance, rest assured that most teen athletes who lift weights see improvements in their game, not declines.

Balancing Tip: If you play sports, focus on a strength training routine that complements your specific athletic needs. Exercises that build explosive power, speed, and core stability will help you perform better on the field or court.

Myth: More Training Equals Faster Gains
(The Dangers of Overtraining)

It's natural to think that the more you train, the faster you'll build muscle. But overtraining is actually one of the biggest mistakes beginners make. Your body needs time to recover in order to grow.

When you overtrain—lifting too often, without enough rest—your body doesn't have the chance to repair muscle fibres, which can slow progress and even lead to injury.

Overtraining can lead to:

Fatigue: You might start feeling constantly tired, even outside the gym.

Decreased performance: You may notice that your lifts start getting weaker instead of stronger, despite training more often.

Increased risk of injury: Without proper recovery, your muscles, tendons, and joints are more vulnerable to strain and injury.

Mental burnout: Training too much can lead to a lack of motivation and mental exhaustion, making it harder to stay on track.

How to avoid overtraining:

Listen to your body: If you feel unusually tired, sore, or mentally drained, it's a sign that you may need more rest.

Take rest days: Aim for at least 1-2 full rest days per week, where you avoid intense physical activity.

Prioritise sleep: Sleep is essential for muscle recovery. Teens should aim for 8-10 hours of quality sleep each night to ensure their bodies have enough time to rebuild and repair.

Vary your training: Mix up your workouts so you're not training the same muscles every day. This gives different muscle groups time to recover.

Recovery Tip: Don't underestimate the power of recovery. Taking time off to rest will actually help you build more muscle in the long run. Balance hard work with proper rest for maximum gains.

CHAPTER 7: HOW TO STAY SAFE WHILE LIFTING

Safety should always be your top priority when lifting weights, especially as a teen. While strength training can help you build muscle and boost your confidence, it can also lead to injury if not done correctly. In this chapter, we'll go over key tips to help you lift safely, avoid common mistakes, and recognise when your body needs rest.

Proper Warm-Up Routines and Why They Matter

Warming up is essential before any workout. It prepares your body for the physical demands of lifting and helps prevent injuries by increasing blood flow to your muscles and joints. Skipping a proper warm-up can lead to pulled muscles or joint problems, which can set you back in your training.

Warm-up Tips:

Start with light cardio: 5-10 minutes of light jogging, cycling, or jumping jacks will get your blood flowing and your body ready for heavier work.

Dynamic stretches: Focus on stretches that move your muscles through their full range of motion, like arm circles, leg swings, and hip rotations. This helps loosen up tight muscles.

Warm-up sets: Before jumping into your working sets, do 1-2 sets of your exercise at a lower weight to get used to the movement and focus on proper form.

Why it Matters: A good warm-up reduces the risk of strains, sprains, and other common gym injuries. It also mentally prepares you for the workout ahead, ensuring you're focused and ready to give it your best.

How to Lift Safely and When to Ask for Help

When it comes to lifting weights, form is everything. Lifting with bad technique can put stress on your joints and muscles, increasing the risk of injury. Always prioritise proper form over lifting heavy weights.

Safe Lifting Tips:

Start light: As a beginner, focus on mastering the movement before adding heavy weights. Once your form is solid, gradually increase the weight.

Use a spotter: For heavy lifts like the bench press or squats, always ask someone to spot you. A spotter can help prevent accidents if you get stuck under the weight.

Focus on form: Keep your back straight during exercises like deadlifts and squats, avoid locking your joints, and control the weight throughout the entire movement.

Don't rush: Lifting too fast increases the chances of sloppy form and injuries. Perform each rep with control.

When to Ask for Help: If you're unsure about your form, don't hesitate to ask a coach, trainer, or even a more experienced lifter for advice. It's better to learn the right way than to risk injury.

The Importance of Rest Days and Avoiding Burnout

Rest days are just as important as workout days. Your muscles grow and recover when you rest, so overtraining without proper recovery can lead to burnout and injuries. Teens, especially, need time to recover as their bodies are still developing.

Why Rest Matters:

Muscle Recovery: Rest days allow your muscles to repair the small tears caused by lifting. Without enough rest, you risk overtraining and stalling your progress.

Preventing Burnout: Overtraining can lead to physical and mental fatigue. Giving your body time to recover ensures you stay motivated and energised for your next workout.

Recognizing and Dealing with Injuries

Even with the best precautions, injuries can happen. It's important to recognize when something is wrong and take action early to prevent further damage.

Common Lifting Injuries:

Muscle Strains: Overstretching or overworking a muscle can cause strains.

Joint Pain: Lifting with poor form can stress your knees, shoulders, or elbows.

Back Pain: Improper technique during exercises like deadlifts or squats can lead to lower back pain.

How to Handle an Injury:

Stop training: If you feel sharp pain, stop immediately. Continuing to push through can make the injury worse.

Rest and ice: Give the affected area time to recover. Ice can help reduce swelling and pain.

See a doctor: If the pain persists or worsens, seek medical advice. It's always better to be safe than sorry.

CHAPTER 7: SETTING LONG-TERM GOALS AND BUILDING A FIT LIFESTYLE

Now that you've learned the fundamentals of strength training, nutrition, and safety, it's time to think beyond just the next workout or the upcoming weeks. Building muscle and staying fit is a long-term commitment that can bring incredible benefits, not just now, but for the rest of your life. In this chapter, we'll explore how to set realistic goals, track your progress, and integrate fitness into your daily routine for lasting results.

Setting SMART Goals for Fitness Progress

When it comes to fitness, vague goals like "get stronger" or "build muscle" can leave you without a clear direction. That's why it's important to set SMART goals: goals that are Specific, Measurable, Achievable, Relevant, and Time-bound. This approach helps you stay focused and motivated, breaking down your long-term aspirations into manageable steps.

Here's what SMART goals might look like:

Specific: Instead of saying "I want to get stronger," say "I want to add 20 pounds to my bench press in the next three months."

Measurable: Track your progress by keeping records of how much weight you're lifting, how many reps you can do, or your muscle measurements.

Achievable: Be realistic with your goals. It's great to aim high, but setting goals that are too ambitious can lead to frustration. Start with smaller, achievable goals and build from there.

Relevant: Ensure your goals align with your overall fitness aspirations. If your primary goal is to build muscle, focus on strength training rather than cardio-heavy routines.

Time-bound: Set deadlines for your goals, such as "I want to gain 5 pounds of muscle in six months."

By following the SMART method, you'll have a clear roadmap for success and a greater sense of accomplishment when you hit your targets.

Tracking Progress with Journals, Apps, and Photos

To reach your long-term goals, you need to track your progress regularly. This not only keeps you accountable but also shows you how far you've come, which can be incredibly motivating.

Tracking Methods:

Workout Journals: Keep a notebook where you write down every workout, including the exercises, sets, reps, and weights used. This helps you see week-to-week improvements and know when it's time to increase the intensity.

Apps: Fitness apps like MyFitnessPal, Strong, or Jefit allow you to log your workouts and meals, track your progress, and even set reminders for workouts. They can be a great tool for staying organised.

Progress Photos: Sometimes, the mirror doesn't show changes as clearly as you'd like. Take progress photos every month to visually track muscle growth and changes in your body. It's one of the best ways to see how far you've come.

No matter which method you choose, consistently tracking your progress is key to staying on top of your goals and making adjustments when necessary.

Balancing Muscle-Building with Sports, School, and Other Priorities

As a teen, you're juggling a lot—school, sports, social activities, and more. Finding the right balance between strength training and your other commitments is crucial for long-term success. Overloading yourself can lead to burnout, while neglecting your fitness routine can hinder progress.

Tips for Balance:

Time Management: Set a weekly schedule that includes both your workouts and other priorities. Treat your workout time as non-negotiable, just like you would with homework or practice.

Short but Effective Workouts: You don't need to spend hours in the gym to see results. Full-body workouts or split routines lasting 45-60 minutes are effective if you stay focused and work hard.

Adjusting for Sports Seasons: During your sports season, you might need to scale back on heavy lifting to avoid overtraining. Focus on maintaining strength with shorter, lighter sessions and pick up the intensity during the off-season.

Rest and Recovery: Make sure you're getting enough rest, especially if you're balancing multiple activities. Sleep and proper nutrition are key to keeping your energy levels up and your muscles growing.

Finding the right balance between fitness and your other priorities will help you stay consistent without burning out.

Developing a Lifelong Love of Fitness and Wellness

One of the most important takeaways from your fitness journey is learning to view exercise not as a chore, but as a lifelong habit. When you approach fitness with the mindset of improving your overall health and well-being, it becomes something you enjoy and look forward to.

Tips for Building a Fit Lifestyle:

Find What You Love: While strength training is a great foundation, it's important to mix it up with activities you enjoy. Whether it's swimming, running, hiking, or team sports, incorporating different forms of exercise keeps things interesting and helps you stay active.

Make Fitness Social: Working out with friends or joining a sports team can make fitness more enjoyable and motivating. Surround yourself with people who support your goals and share your interest in staying healthy.

Stay Curious: Fitness is always evolving, and there's always more to learn. Whether it's trying new exercises, experimenting with different training styles, or diving deeper into nutrition, maintaining a curious mindset keeps things exciting.

Set New Challenges: As you reach your initial goals, set new ones to keep pushing yourself. Whether it's trying to deadlift more weight, running a 5k, or mastering a new skill like handstands, continuous improvement will keep you motivated for years to come.

Building a fit lifestyle isn't just about lifting weights—it's about embracing physical activity as a core part of who you are. When you view fitness this way, it becomes a rewarding and sustainable part of your life.

You've made it through the essential steps to build muscle, grow stronger, and set yourself up for a lifetime of fitness success.

Whether you're just starting out or already have some experience, this book has given you the tools, knowledge, and strategies to take your strength training and muscle-building to the next level.

But remember—fitness isn't just about what you do in the gym or how much muscle you can build. It's about creating a lifestyle that promotes physical health, mental well-being, and self-confidence. The strength you develop goes beyond your muscles; it affects your ability to take on challenges, persevere through difficulties, and build discipline that will serve you in every area of life.

What's Next?

Now, it's up to you to put everything you've learned into action. Here's a roadmap to keep in mind as you move forward:

Stick to the Basics: Continue mastering the core exercises and progressively challenge yourself with new goals.

Track Your Progress: Use your journal, photos, or apps to measure your growth and celebrate small wins along the way.

Stay Safe: Always prioritise proper form, rest, and recovery to avoid injury and burnout.

Eat Well: Keep fueling your body with nutritious foods to support your muscle growth and overall health.

Keep Learning: Fitness is an ongoing journey. Stay curious, explore new techniques, and always be open to improving.

Final Thoughts

As a teenager, you have a unique advantage: you're starting early. The habits you build now will lay the foundation for a strong, healthy, and confident future. Whether your goal is to build muscle, boost athletic performance, or simply feel better in your own skin, the knowledge you've gained here is the first step on your lifelong fitness journey.

The most important thing to remember is to enjoy the process. Results take time, but consistency will pay off. Embrace the challenge, celebrate your progress, and most importantly, have fun with it.

This is your journey, and it's just beginning. Now go out there, crush your goals, and become the strongest version of yourself—both in and out of the gym. The future is in your hands, and you've got everything it takes to succeed.

Stay strong, stay disciplined, and remember: you're capable of more than you think.

Printed in Great Britain
by Amazon

52821364R00036